In the Lakelan
of Beatrix ~~Potter~~

Lindsey Porter

Beatrix Potter by Delmar Banner, oil on canvas, 1938.
© National Portrait Gallery, London

Published by
Guidelines Book & Sales
11 Belmont Road, Ipstones, Stoke on Trent ST10 2JN
☎ 07971 990649 email: author.porter@gmail.com

ISBN 978-1-84306-410-7

© **Lindsey Porter 2012**

Photo Acknowledgements
Page1: NPG 3635, Beatrix Potter by Delmar Banner, oil on canvas, 1938. © National Portrait Gallery, London; p13 © National Trust Picture Library/Geoffrey Frosh; p18 top © National Trust Picture Library/ Alex Black; Front cover & p31 Caroline Watson; Back cover left & bottom and p32 © The World of Beatrix Potter Attraction

Printed by Information Press Ltd, Eynsham, Oxford

Key to map

Map numbers relate to identified properties in the text. The map is for this purpose only and not for use as a road atlas.

1 Wray Castle	11 Esthwaite Water
2 Lindeth Howe Country House Hotel	12 Tarn Hows
3 Holehird	13 Troutbeck Park Farm
4 Hill Top	14 Brockhole
5 Castle Farm, Near Sawrey	15 The Armitt Museum
6 Beatrix Potter Gallery	16 Holbeck Ghyll Hotel
7 Old Court House	17 Loughrigg Tarn
8 Tilberthwaite Ghyll	18 Loughrigg Terrace
9 Ees Wyke Country Hotel	19 Yew Tree Farm
10 Grasmere	20 World of Beatrix Potter

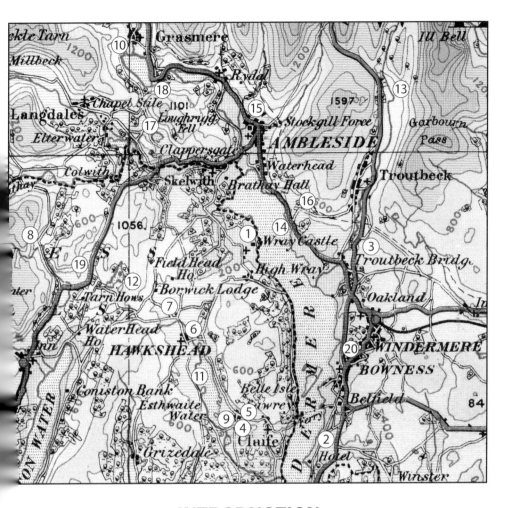

INTRODUCTION

For many of us, I suspect, we have associated Beatrix Potter (28/7/1866 – 22/12/1943) with the Lake District through her home Hill Top Farm at Near Sawrey, the Gallery in Hawkshead and the visitor attraction – The World of Beatrix Potter – in Bowness. Having grown up with her lovely childhood stories it is easy to link the recreated scenes of Mrs Tiggywinkle and friends at Bowness with what is best in our memories and association with the Lake District.

Our peripheral knowledge of Beatrix Potter came suddenly back into focus with the release in January 2007 of the film *Miss Potter*. Here was the story of a young woman, nudging her mid-life years who fell in love and tragically lost it before it had blossomed. Finding solace in the purchase of Hill Top Farm, she embarked upon another life, centred in the Lakes, leaving behind London and her childhood home.

Many of her books followed, before she found another love and eventually marriage to William Heelis in 1913. At this point her output of 24 childrens' stories largely ended. *Miss Potter* also focused on her life as an aspiring author and the profound way in which she influenced our enjoyment of the Lakes today.

Through her sensitivity to the cause of protection of the fells and the traditional way of life she found there, she used her wealth to purchase many farms and fells. Today, these are now in the hands of the National Trust, who continue her vision of protection and the promotion of traditional values she encouraged so much.

Although the Lakes have attracted many authors and poets, it remains synonymous with the work of William Wordsworth. Yet the work of Beatrix Potter has found an incredible worldwide following, not least amongst the overseas visitors who arrive in large numbers each year to find out more about the woman, her life and stories with which they have grown up.

Widely acclaimed in her own lifetime, she sought to limit its affect upon her everyday life. Managing her farms, her life became focused in a different direction to the escapism (if that is the right word) of her story books. The interest in her today is significant and one wonders what she would have made of it. Perhaps there is an element of her legacy which has yet to be used to its full potential.

Hill Top helps us focus on the need to protect the fells and the traditional way of life she felt was so important, portraying what she did and how we can continue to promote her ideals. The need for a sustainable economy for our Lakeland hill farmers, the real guardians of our fells, has never been greater. Providing that sustainability could be the best way in which we could respond to the enjoyment Beatrix Potter gave and continues to give, to so many of us. Understanding what the problems are gives visitors the chance to contribute to the cause she espoused with such passion. Assisting the National Trust helps them in their work to this end.

Some of the properties associated with Beatrix are open to the public and some offer accommodation. Contact details are provided in each case. In recognition of the importance of the work and benevolence of Beatrix Potter, the headquarters of the National Trust in Great Western Village, Swindon, is known as "Heelis', her married surname.

For other accommodation than that shown herein, contact local Tourist Information Centres, eg Ambleside on ☎ 015394 32582 or The Youth Hostels Association Contact Centre ☎ 01629 592700.

Lakeland Holidays

Wray Castle, Low Wray, is on the west side of Derwentwater, opposite The Low Wood Hotel on the Windermere–Ambleside road (1). Here Beatrix Potter stayed on her first Lake District holiday, when aged 16, in 1882. Low Wray Church, built adjacent to Wray Castle lodge was the living of Canon Rawnsley, one of the founders of The National Trust. Rawnsley must have made quite an impact on Beatrix. Wray Castle is now owned by The National Trust and is open to the public. The architecture is Gothic Revival, a 19th century style invoking medieval architecture, which was very much in vogue in Victorian times. Rawnsley was only here for five years before moving to Crosthwaite Church near Keswick.

Above: Wray Castle (1). **Bottom:** Low Wray Church (1), the living of Canon Rawnsley.

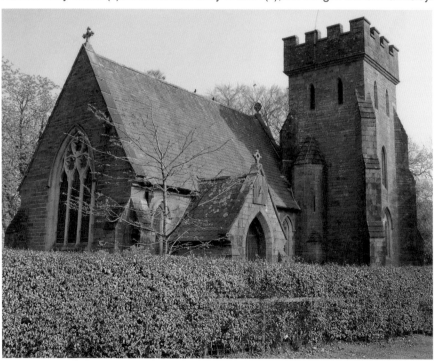

Above and overleaf: Lindeth Howe Country House Hotel & Restaurant (2). Longtail Hill, Windermere, Cumbria LA23 3JF

☎ 015394 45759 www.lindeth-howe.co.uk

Now a 4★ hotel, Beatrix Potter spent some of her holidays here. She later purchased it in 1919 for her mother, Helen, who died in 1932. *The Tales of Pigling Bland* (1913) and *Timmy Tiptoes* (1911) were illustrated here. It is situated to the south of Bowness. Beatrix was using her second name. Her first name was Helen after her mother and she was called Beatrix to avoid confusion.

Above: Lindeth Howe Country House Hotel (see also p 7).

Above and opposite: Holehird [not open to the public] (3).
Now a Cheshire Home, situated 1.5 miles up the A592 Patterdale road from Windermere, (Sat Nav LA23 1NP). The Potters twice rented this house for their extended summer holiday. The 17 acre hillside gardens are now open to the public, in the care of the Lakeland Horticultural Society.

Left: Fawe Park [not open to the public]. Situated at the north end of the west side of Derwentwater.

The Potters stayed in the Lake District for their 3-month holidays from c.1882. This area was the setting for the *Tales of Squirrel Nutkin* (1903); *Benjamin Bunny* (1904), which features Fawe Park; and *Mrs Tiggy-Winkle* (1905). The walk up the ridge of Cat Bells was the setting for the latter. Derwent Isle in Derwentwater is Owl Island in *The Tale of Squirrel Nutkin* and the book is also set in The Newlands Valley and on Cat Bells.

Below: The public path through Fawe Park affords a glimpse of the house. It commences at Nichol End, near to the jetty. The path continues down to the bottom of the lake and on to the Keswick–Honister road, where you can get a boat back to Nichol End in the summer.

Near Sawrey

Hill Top, Near Sawrey (4)

Three months after the sudden death of Norman Warne – her publisher (precisely one month after Beatrix accepted his proposal of marriage, on 25th August, 1905) Beatrix purchased Hill Top Farm, Near Sawrey. It was to be her home until her marriage to local solicitor William Heelis in 1913. She extended it in 1906. Seven of her books are set here, including *Tom Kitten* (1907) and *Samuel Whiskers* (1908). The house is virtually as it was when Beatrix passed away. Here some of her best titles were written. Following her death (on 22nd December 1943), Hill Top was bequeathed to The National Trust.

Visiting the house: ☎ 015394 36269, or hilltop@nationaltrust.org.uk. The house is shut from November to mid-February and on Fridays except Good Friday. The Trust has a shop here by the garden gate ☎ 01539 436801. It is open daily except from Xmas to mid-February when it is closed. It is worth bearing in mind that this is a very popular attraction and visitors sometimes have to wait to enter the house. Advance booking is not available. The house is behind the Tower Bank Arms in the middle of the village.

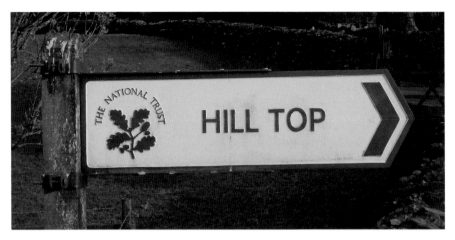

Two views of Near Sawrey from near the Tower Arms, with a signpost to Hill Top.

Hill Top Farm, showing Beatrix Potter's bedroom.
© National Trust Picture Library/Geoffrey Frosh

The Tower Bank Arms, Near Sawrey (4), which features in *The Tale of Jemima Puddle-Duck* (1908), now owned by The National Trust.

Two views of Buckle Yeat Guest House, just below the Tower Bank Arms, Near Sawrey. (4) It features in *The Pie and the Patty-pan (1905)*, *The Tale of Tom Kitten* (1907) and *The Tale of Pigling Bland* (1913). The model is of Mr McGregor from *The Tale of Peter Rabbit* (1902). The house is now a 4★ silver guest house; Near Sawrey, Hawkshead, Ambleside LA22 0LF ☎ 015394 36446. www.buckle-yeat.co.uk

Above: Castle Farm, Near Sawrey, purchased in 1909 (5). It was the home of Beatrix Potter after her marriage to William Heelis in 1913 (it is not open to the public). Beatrix farmed both Castle Farm and Hill Top Farm. **Below:** a corner of the village (properties not open to the public),

Hawkshead Today

The National Trust's Beatrix Potter Gallery, Main Street, Hawkshead, LA22 0NS, ☎ 015394 36355 (6).

This was the solicitor's office of Beatrix Potter's husband, William Heelis. Exhibitions are held here of original illustrations from her books and other paintings and sketches. It is well worth a visit. Here you can learn more about her work as a local farmer and her connections with the National Trust. The building dates from the 17th century and is of interest in itself. Close to the Gallery is the Trust's shop (see p 18). Hawkshead is the setting for *The Tale of Johnny Townmouse* (1918).

The office of Mr Heelis, Beatrix's husband, now the Beatrix Potter Gallery, Hawkshead. © National Trust Picture Library/Alex Black

Two more village scenes showing Beatrix Potter giftshops.

Above: The Kings Arms Hotel. **Below:** The Methodist church and the Minstrel's Gallery (6)

Hawkshead Parish Church and former Grammar School. William Wordsworth was a pupil here (6). William carved his name on one of the desks, which may still be seen. The museum is open from 1 April to 31 September. ☎ 015394 36735.

Above: This is the Old Court House, the only surviving wing of the former Hawkshead Hall and open to the public (7). **Below:** the present Hawkshead Hall (not open to the public) with the Old Court House beyond.

The Monk Coniston Purchase

In 1930, The Monk Coniston Estate, consisting of the Hall, 14 farms and 4,000 acres of land plus various cottages was put up for sale, having been bought privately in June 1908. The Hall was bought privately again, eventually being aquired by the National Trust in 1945. It is now leased by Holiday Fellowship, Britain's biggest walking and leisure activity provider; reservations: ☎ 470 8558 or reservations@hfholidays.co.uk

The estate farms were aquired by Beatrix Potter who sold-on half of the farms at the purchase price to the National Trust.

Upon her death, the remaining farms, together with Castle Farm and Hill Top Farm at Near Sawrey, Troutbeck Park Farm etc were bequeathed to the Trust.

The land put up for sale included the following farms:

Atkinson Ground Farm, Coniston; Far End Farm, Coniston; High Tilberthwaite Farm, Coniston; High Yewdale Farm, Coniston; How Head Farm, Coniston; Low Hall Garth Farm, Coniston; Low Yewdale Farm, Coniston; Yew Tree Farm, Coniston, (including Tarn Hows); Holme Ground Farm, Skelwith; Oxenfell Farm, Skelwith; Stang End Farm, Skelwith; High Park Farm, Skelwith.

Right: This view of the Tilberthwaite Ghyll area typifies the hill farm land which Beatrix felt so passionate about protecting. It is situated just north of Coniston, off the Ambleside road (8). The track visible on the left is not a right of way, but a path climbs up to the left of it, over Low Fell. It then drops down towards Greenburn Beck before contouring around to Low Hall Garth (see above), south of Little Langdale Tarn

.

Other Connections

Just outside Hawkshead are three lakes associated with Beatrix Potter: Esthwaite Water, Moss Eccles Tarn and Tarn Hows. The Ees Wyke Country Hotel (5★) is situated on the west side of Near Sawrey, overlooking Esthwaite Water (9). This was another holiday home of the Potters, then known as Lakefield.
Ees Wyke Country Hotel, Near Sawrey, Hawkshead, LA22 0JZ,
☎ 015394 36393 Email: mail@eeswyke.co.uk

Above: A path goes north from Near Sawrey towards Claife Heights and after about 1 mile passes Moss Eccles Tarn. Beatrix Potter kept a rowing boat on Moss Eccles Tarn. You can still capture the tranquility she would have experienced by hiring a boat on Grasmere (10). The hire centre is just west of Grasmere village.

Right: Esthwaite Water (11) is the setting for *The Tale of Mr Jeremy Fisher* (1906).

Lovely Tarn Hows (12) purchased by Beatrix in 1930 as part of the Monk Coniston Estate and conveyed on to The National Trust. It is arguably the most attractive and popular part of Lakeland. The lake was created by JG Marshall of Monk Coniston Hall. He built a small dam at the southern end which raised the water sufficiently to flood the land around three small lakes to create the current one. The National Trust maintains an adjacent carpark and there is a path around the water. Opposite (top): Tarn Hows, viewed from the water's edge.

To the west and below Tarn Hows, on the Coniston- Ambleside road is another lovely lake, Yew Tree Tarn. This is not owned by the National Trust, but the backcloth of fells, seen here and centred on Holme Fell are. They abut Oxen Fell Farm to the north and Holme Ground Farm and Tilberthwaite to the west.

Troutbeck Park Farm on the Trout Beck, situated a couple of miles north of Troutbeck village, a hill farm purchased from book royalties in 1923 (13). Beatrix ran it herself from 1926, employing George Walker, the brother-in-law of Tom Storey, who ran Hill Top Farm. Here was the setting for *The Fairy Caravan* (1929). She built the detached house on the right for him.

Below: Brockhole, Windermere, (14) showing the Terrace. The former home of Beatrix's cousin, Edith Gaddum, it is now the National Park Visitor Centre. It is situated approximately halfway between Windermere and Ambleside on a site looking down onto the lake. There are trails down to the water, where a new jetty has been built for the steamer traffic. The house was built in 1897–1900 as a 'summer house' for WHA Gaddum, a Manchester silk merchant.

Beatrix came here for the Gaddum's Golden Wedding in 1936.

The Armitt Museum, Ambleside (15).
In 1943, Beatrix left her collection of over 450 fungi, natural history and archaeological watercolours to the Armitt Museum Library. It is situated a little to the north of the Bridge House and on the opposite side of the road.

Armitt Museum, Rydal Road, Ambleside LA22 9BL
☎ 015394 31212

Miss Potter Locations

The Holbeck Ghyll Hotel (16), where Renée Zellweger and others stayed whilst filming in the Lake District. It is north of Windermere village and was the home of Lord Lonsdale. He is the man after whom the Lonsdale belt in boxing is named.

Holbeck Ghyll Hotel, Holbeck Road, Windermere LA23 1LU
☎ 015394 32375 email: stay@holbeckghyll.com

Loughrigg Tarn (17). Both this and Loughrigg Terrace, (18) (high above Grasmere, but an easy walk, looking down on Grasmere), feature in the film. There are some superb views from the Terrace

Yew Tree Farm, on the Coniston–Ambleside road (19). It sells 'Heritage Meat' products based upon Herdwick sheep and Belted Galloway cattle. One of the best known farms in the Lake District, it also offers high quality Bed and Breakfast accommodation. The farm dates from 1693 and some of Beatrix Potter's furnishings remain as she left it. She bought it at the Monk Coniston sale in 1930 and it doubled for Hill Top Farm in the film *Miss Potter.* On the left is an unusual survivor, an old Spinning Gallery. The farm is owned by the National Trust.

Yew Tree Farm, Coniston LA21 8DF
☎ 015394 41433
email: info@yewtree-farm.co.uk
Five★ Gold Award, Visit Britain

Photo: Caroline Watson, Yew Tree Farm

The World of Beatrix Potter Attraction (20)

This very popular attraction, a Cumbria Tourism Awards Winner, is a unique portrayal of the authoress's characters. The attraction covers 23 of her books to enchant both young and old. This is one of the top tourist attractions in the Lakes other than the fells themselves. There are recreated scenes such as Mrs Tiggy-Winkle in her kitchen; Peter Rabbit in Mr McGregor's garden and Jemima Puddle-Duck in a woodland glade.

There is a Beatrix Potter shop selling Peter Rabbit gifts, plus a tea room and the Miss Potter room, which portrays the life and times of the authoress. Allow 45-60 minutes for your visit.

The World of Beatrix Potter Attraction, Crag Brow, Bowness on Windermere LA23 3BX. ☎ 0844 504 1233 or information@hop-skip-jump.com

Left: Scenes at the attractions **Right:** Mr McGregor's garden